WOLVES
& THEIR RELATIVES

Erik D. Stoops & Dagmar Fertl

Sterling Publishing Co., Inc.
New York

Library of Congress Cataloging-in-Publication Data

Stoops, Erik D., 1966–
    Wolves & their relatives / Erik D. Stoops & Dagmar Fertl.
        p.   cm.
    Includes index.
    Summary: Questions and answers introduce the habits and lifestyles of wolves
and their relatives.
    ISBN 0-8069-0926-9
    1. Wolves—Miscellanea—Juvenile literature.   [1. Wolves—Miscellanea.
2. Questions and answers.]   I. Fertl, Dagmar.   II. Title.
QL737.C22S78   1997   96-35794
599.74′442—dc20   CIP
                                                                                        AC

Designed by Judy Morgan

1   3   5   7   9   10   8   6   4   2

First paperback edition published in 1998 by
Sterling Publishing Company, Inc.
387 Park Avenue South, New York, N.Y. 10016
© 1997 by Erik D. Stoops & Dagmar Fertl
Distributed in Canada by Sterling Publishing
% Canadian Manda Group, One Atlantic Avenue, Suite 105
Toronto, Ontario, Canada M6K 3E7
Distributed in Great Britain and Europe by Cassell PLC
Wellington House, 125 Strand, London WC2R 0BB, England
Distributed in Australia by Capricorn Link (Australia) Pty Ltd.
P.O. Box 6651, Baulkham Hills, Business Centre, NSW 2153, Australia
Printed in Hong Kong

Sterling ISBN 0-8069-0926-9 Trade
0-8069-1791-1 Paper

CONTENTS

HOW WOLVES LIVE

The wolf has long been thought to be a mystical and secretive creature, but it has actually been well studied by scientists. The wolf is the ancestor of the family dog. It lives in many parts of the world. Where does a wolf live? What is a pack? Why do wolves howl? These are just a few of the questions you will find answered in this chapter.

◀ **Wolves and their relatives may be found in most continents.**

▶ **If you look closely, you can see the large canine teeth of this coyote. It uses these teeth to hold onto its food.**

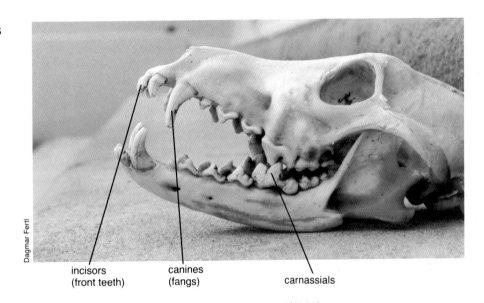

Dagmar Fertl

incisors (front teeth)   canines (fangs)   carnassials

What family of animals does the wolf belong to?

The wolf is a member of the dog family. This family also includes foxes, jackals, and coyotes. They are called **canids** (kay-nidz).

Is a wolf warm- or cold-blooded?

A wolf is a mammal. All mammals are warm-blooded, have hair or fur, bear live young, nurse their babies with milk, and breathe air with lungs.

To what are dogs related?

Dogs are related to cats, bears, raccoons, and sea lions. Scientists list them in the order of animals called **carnivores** (car-nuh-vorz). They each have four special teeth adapted to slice meat.

Where are wolves found?

Wolves and other wild dog species live in almost every country in the world.

Dr. Bernd Würsig

© Monty Sloan

▲ Gray wolves are on the move night and day, while the red wolf is more active at night.

▶ Maned wolves live in pairs, not in groups.

◀ The red fox is one of the members of the canid family. It is one of the most common species of wild dog.

What is a pack?

A wolf pack is like a family. Each pack is led by one male and one female who make the decisions and face most of the dangers. The lower-ranking wolves are also important to the pack since they help hunt and feed and take care of the pups.

Erik Stoops

Do wolves always get along with each other?

No, wolves are territorial. They mark their area and defend it against other packs. When the dominant animal in the group is old, sick, or injured it can be hard for the leader to keep the others in line. Also, subordinates often challenge or test the dominant animal to try to become the leader.

▼ A wolf will sometimes roll on its back when higher-ranking wolves approach it.

What is submission?

When one animal obeys another animal, this is called submission. Pet dogs often show submissive behavior to their master. There are two types of submission: active and passive. Active submission is when a dominant animal forces another animal to obey her/him. Wolves will do this by pushing each other down to the ground. Passive submission is when a defeated or subordinate animal lowers itself to the ground without being forced by the dominant animal. By acting submissive in a fight situation, an animal can avoid serious injury.

▶ The wolf that has his front legs across the top of the other wolf's back is the dominant one.

© Monty Sloan

© Monty Sloan

7

▲ The animal that is subordinate is the one with the ears laid back on the head.

▲ A wolf pack is very organized. Each wolf in the pack knows its rank and how to act around the other pack members.

▶ The wolf that is crouching is saying, "You're the boss."

How long does a wolf live?

Wolves and their relatives live for about seven to ten years. According to scientists, the oldest wolf known was 17 years old.

▶ **Pack life is important to the survival of adults and pups alike.**

▶ **Wolves are social animals. They tend to live in packs. Lone wolves are usually younger animals looking for a mate and territory.**

How many wolves are in a pack?

A pack of wolves can have as few as two or as many as 20 members. Usually there are about six or seven wolves in a group. The pack size depends on many different things, such as whether the wolves eat large animals, the age of the wolves in the pack, and how much food is around in their territory.

▲ **This wolf may be howling to call its other pack members, who could be many miles away.**

Why do wolves howl?

Wolves howl for many different reasons. When they are spread out, pack members will howl to stay in touch with the rest of the group. Did you know that wolves can tell each other to stay out of their home area when they howl?

▲ **Wolves can recognize each other when they howl since each animal sounds a little different.**

What are the ancestors of wolves?

Wolves and their relatives are descended from small, insect-eating mammals called *Miacidae* (my-Ee-si-dee), which lived during the time of the dinosaurs. About 50 million years ago, some of the insect eaters evolved into dogs.

► The *Cynodicitis* was an ancestor of modern wolves. It had a long body and short legs.

Frank Barath

Are any wolves extinct?

No. There are no extinct wolves or wild dogs.

► The Tasmanian wolf, which is now thought to be extinct, looked like a dog, but it was a marsupial. The Tasmanian wolf was more closely related to a kangaroo than a wolf. This animal had a unique color pattern that made it look as if it were half tiger and half wolf.

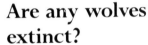

Frank Barath

11

Where do wolves live?

Wolves and their relatives are found living all around the world except in Antarctica and some islands, including New Zealand, Madagascar, and the Philippines. Wild dogs make their homes in areas ranging from the Arctic tundra, forests, deserts, and grasslands to tropical regions.

Steve Fritts/U.S. Fish and Wildlife Service

© Monty Sloan

▲ Wolves are very good at digging holes with their large paws. It only takes them a few hours to dig a hole to use as a den.

▲ A den is a place to go to get out of the rain, to sleep, and to raise puppies.

The same den may be used year after year by the same wolves.

How large is a wolf den?

A typical wolf's den entrance has been described as being 14–25 inches (36–64 cm) across and oval in shape. The tunnel into it is about 6–14 feet (2–4 m) long. Wolf dens are located in high ground areas with water nearby.

▶ **This rocky overhang provides shady shelter for this dingo pup, an Australian relative of the wolf.**

P. Thompson

Do wolves hibernate?

No, and its only relative that does is the raccoon dog. This wild dog from Russia and northern Asia looks like a raccoon because of its tail and face mask. By hibernating, the raccoon dog avoids the cold, harsh winter.

M. Cukierski/American Society of Mammalogists.

◀ **The raccoon dog is the only wolf relative that hibernates.**

13

THE WOLF'S BODY

The wolf's body is adapted for pursuing other animals for food, as well as for surviving in the environment where it lives. Imagine having powerful muscles to chase prey, sharp teeth to tear, kill and eat it, and big ears to hear everything. How many teeth does a wolf have? Why is its fur important? These are just some of the questions in this chapter.

How many teeth does a wolf have?

◄ **The wolf is a smart animal that seems to learn things quickly and that has a good memory. These qualities help it survive.**

Wolves and most of their relatives have 42 teeth. The exception is the bat-eared dog, which has 4–8 more teeth. The **canine** (k-9) teeth, or fangs, hold on to the food. The **incisors** (in-size-erz) tear meat off bones and the **carnassials** (car-nah-see-alls) cut meat into smaller pieces as your molars do.

▶ **If you look closely you can see the very sharp teeth and powerful jaws of this gray wolf.**

© Monty Sloan

© Monty Sloan

How many toes does a wolf have?

All canids have five toes on each of their front feet, except for the African wild dog, which has four toes. All canids have four toes on their back feet.

▶ **A canid's claws always stick out. A cat is able to retract (pull back) its claws.**

Julian Center for Science and Education

What is a dew claw?

The fifth toe on the front foot is very small. It is located above the foot pad on the inside of the leg. This toe is called a dew claw.

▶ **Look at the back of this dingo's front leg and you can see its dew claw, which sticks out.**

Laurie Corbett/Courtesy of Colin Groves

16

Is it true that wolves walk on tiptoes?

Yes. The ankle joint is very easy to see; look halfway up the leg where it juts out. The ankle in a canid is called a hock.

▼ Scientists can tell that a canid has made this footprint in the mud by the claw marks in the track.

▲ The majority of wild dogs, like the gray wolf, have long legs and muscular bodies to help them run fast, as well as an impressive set of teeth to kill and eat their prey. Members of the dog family also share slender muzzles and long, fluffy tails.

17

How many types of fur do wolves have?

Wolves and their relatives have two types of "fur coat" that they wear at the same time. The undercoat (the short fur closest to the skin) is soft and keeps the wolf warm. The overcoat is made up of long hairs, which act as a weather barrier. This would be like wearing a sweater that keeps you warm, and a jacket over the sweater to protect you from the rain, wind or snow.

Do wolves shed these fur coats?

Yes, wolves can shed their fur once a year. Wolves' bodies respond to changing amounts of daylight. For example, summer has longer days, triggering various hormonal changes.

▼ **When this wolf sheds its warm, fluffy undercoat of fur, its remaining fur will be the same color.**

▲ **Outer wolf fur with its long hairs is called the overcoat. It protects the animal from rain and snow.**

◄ **Gray wolves may have black, white, or gray fur.**

Carter Niemaier/U.S. Department of Agriculture

© Monty Sloan

© Monty Sloan

18

Do any wolves change color during the winter?

Wolves don't, but their relatives, the Arctic fox and the Corsac fox go through color changes during the winter. Arctic foxes are gray during summer and blue or white in the winter.

▲ (Above and top right) Arctic foxes can be either blue or white during the winter.

▶ By curling up and tucking its tail over its face, this wolf can keep itself warm.

Are there any other ways a wolf can keep warm?

Yes. Besides having two types of fur, the wolf can use its tail to keep warm. It does this by tucking its tail over its face.

Do wolves sweat?

Wolves pant if they get too hot, but according to scientists, the only sweating they can do is through their footpads. Wolves can drink a lot of water and even wade when they get too hot.

▶ **This thirsty wolf is getting a refreshing drink of water. Water is important to every living animal.**

© Monty Sloan

When do wolves sleep?

Wild dogs tend to rest during the hottest times of the day. For desert-dwelling canids, this means that they sleep for most of the day when it is hot and hunt at night when it is cooler. Wolves hunt at any time of the day or night.

Do any wolves live in the desert?

Yes, the Mexican wolf is a desert dweller. Many species of fox, such as the sand fox, also live in the desert. All foxes that live in deserts are small but have huge ears. Big ears can keep an animal cool. Animals that live in the desert also have light-colored fur.

K. Kutunidisz/American Society of Mammalogists

▲ **This is a Ruppell's fox, also known as a sand fox. It lives in the deserts of northern Africa.**

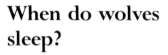

20

▲ Did you know that wolves take naps? Wolves spend a good part of their day resting.

▲ The Cape fox rests during the day because it is too hot for it to do anything else.

◄ An important part of sleeping is stretching. This Mexican wolf probably just woke up from a nap.

How fast can a wolf run?

Gray wolves can usually run for a few hours at about 7–8 miles (11–13 km) per hour without getting tired, while foxes trot along at about 4–8 miles (6.4–13 km) per hour. Wolves can sprint as fast as 35–40 miles (56–64 km) per hour for short distances.

© Monty Sloan

▲ The gray wolf uses more energy when it runs through the snow than it does running on dirt and leaves.

Heather Bell

▲ The swift fox got its name for its speed. Swift foxes can run over 40 miles (64 km) per hour for short distances.

Wildlife World Zoo

▲ African wild dogs can chase animals for as long as 3½ miles (5.6 km), running about 30 miles (48 km) per hour.

▼ The culpeo (cool-pay-oh) runs fast—chasing food and playmates.

Warren E. Johnson

Do wolves ever get sick?

Like other animals, wolves can get sick. Diseases like rabies and distemper can kill wolves and their relatives by making them too weak to hunt for food. These diseases can spread quickly and have been blamed for the deaths of many wild dogs.

What is rabies?

Rabies is a virus that infects only mammals. The virus is passed through the saliva to a wound. It takes about 2–4 weeks before the virus makes its way to the brain. The infected animal starts to lose interest in eating and drinking. It can have a hard time moving around, will cry out for no apparent reason, and drool a lot of saliva. The animal dies shortly afterwards.

© Monty Sloan

◄ This wolf is scratching an itch caused by a pesky flea or tick.

▼ Rabies is a deadly disease that has killed many canids, such as Patagonian gray foxes, and may even kill humans. The disease makes animals very weak and can even cause them to become paralyzed.

Warren E. Johnson

What is a wolf's digestive system like?

Wolves have sharp teeth that help them hold on to their prey to kill it. The wolf doesn't do much chewing; it swallows its food in large pieces. The food makes its way through the esophagus to the stomach and the intestines. Digestive juices break up the food.

THE WOLF'S SENSES

Imagine that you have the senses of a wolf. Imagine knowing if friend, enemy, or dinner is nearby just by using your sense of smell. Find out how wolves use their senses to receive messages and learn about their surroundings.

◄ **Wild dogs use their keen senses to be alert and aware of their surroundings.**

What color eyes do wolves have?

Adult wolves have orange-yellow eyes. Wolf puppies are born with blue eyes, but their eyes change color at about 3 months of age.

▲ **These little wolf pups have the biggest blue eyes . . .**

▲ **. . . which turn an orangish color as the wolf gets older.**

Can a wolf see in the dark?

Wolves and their relatives can see quite well at night. There is a mirror-like layer in the back of the eyes that reflects light. At night, if you shine a light at a fox, for instance, its eyes will gleam. Foxes hunt mostly at night, and they have vertical pupils in their eyes that open wide at night to allow more light to enter.

▲ **These Bengal foxes don't really have green eyes. What you see is light reflected off a layer at the back of the eye that helps the animal see at night.**

Do wolves have eyelids?

Yes, they actually have three. Two of them are normal eyelids (top and bottom), like people's. The third eyelid is a clear mirror-like layer that slips over the eye, like a contact lens. This third eyelid protects the eye from dust, the way your eyelashes protect your eyes. It may also protect the wolf from snow blindness (temporary blindness caused by the sun's glare magnified by the snow).

Can a wolf taste?

Yes. Scientists have found that wolves are able to taste salty, bitter, acid, and even sweet things like fruit.

How well can a wolf smell?

A wolf uses its nose to sniff out different types of news, such as finding dinner, a mate, or figuring out who's new in the area. Scientists tell us that some wolves have five times the amount of "smelling" cells in their noses as other species of mammals. Wolves can smell strong scents up to 1½ miles (1.5–2 km) away!

▲ **A wolf can usually find a food item before it can see it.**

◀ **A wolf's sense of smell is so good that it can sniff out a meal hidden in the snow.**

26

Why is the wolf's sense of smell so powerful?

If you look at the nose area on the skull of a wolf, you will see what looks like a thin layering of bone throughout the hollow area. Some scientists think this network of bones with cell layers helps wolves to smell so well, while others think that it is a way for the animal to make air it breathes warmer and moister before it gets to the lungs.

▶ The purpose of the tiny bones in the nose area of this coyote skull is still being studied. The cells layered in this bone network probably warm and moisten the air that the wolf breathes, and make the nose even more sensitive to smells.

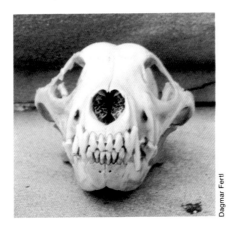

Dagmar Fertl

▼ The bat-eared fox's favorite foods are termites and dung beetles. Its large ears make it easier for the fox to hear those insects and find them.

Why do some wolf relatives have really big ears?

Some wolf relatives have very large ears, like the Fennec fox that lives in the desert and uses his ears to stay cool, and the bat-eared fox, which has a diet mainly of insects.

K. Kutunidisz/American Society of Mammalogists

27

How well do wolves hear?

Wolves have excellent hearing. Not only can they hear sounds from far away, but they can also hear very high frequency sounds we can't hear. A wolf's ears move, so it can focus easily on the direction the sounds are coming from, the way a radio antenna would.

Are a wolf's whiskers important?

Yes! The whiskers are located on the snout. Whiskers help wolves figure out where their food is before they bite into it.

▶ Foxes, like this culpeo, have the longest whiskers of all the canid family.

A. Maggi / Licaone Fund

Warren E. Johnson

◀ The shape of this African wild dog's ears helps it hear well. Cup your hand behind your ear, and you'll hear much better.

What kind of sounds do wolves make?

Wolves make many different sounds, like barking, growling, snarling, whining, yelping, and howling. The dingo is the only canid species that hardly ever barks. Dholes, relatives of the wolf, will sometimes whistle to each other as a form of communication.

How do wolves communicate?

Wolves can express their emotions and "talk" to each other in many ways. These involve the senses of sight, smell, and hearing. The ears, tail, and mouth can be moved in many different ways. Body language also helps to show how wolves feel.

▲ One of the wolves is changing body posture and behavior. The face and tail also provide information on the way the wolf feels.

▲ This wolf can figure out which wolf was here last by sniffing for a scent left behind.

Why do wolves spend so much time sniffing the ground and air?

Animals produce pheromones, chemical messages that can be picked up by the nose. An important message might include who the animal is, and if female, whether she is ready for mating. Wolves can also smell prey for the same reason. Pheromones are like telephone calls or letters, but instead of words, they are smells.

▼ Male wolves can tell when a female is in heat (able to become pregnant) by her smell. Each wolf in the pack might have a different smell. It's like having a name tag. The smell identifies the wolf.

▲ Marking a tree with urine is one way wolves leave messages for each other and mark their territory.

▲ A wolf will sometimes wipe its chin or throat on dead prey. No one really knows why wolves do this. Scientists think it may be a way wolves mark food as theirs.

EATING HABITS

Looking for food is not easy for wolves and their relatives. They eat pretty much anything they find, an important reason many wild dogs have been able to survive through times of little food and human pressures. When do wolves and their relatives hunt alone? When do they hunt in pairs or groups? Did you know that wild dogs eat fruit?

◄ **African wild dogs hunt in packs since their food is big and hard to kill if they try to hunt alone.**

Do wolves hunt together?

Many species of wolves hunt in pairs or groups. Wolves that are hunting large animals, like deer, moose, and gazelles, work together so that they have a better chance of catching their prey.

► **Australian dingoes catch and kill small kangaroos and wallabies. These animals are big enough to feed several dingoes.**

► **When wolves are hunting, they often try to separate a young animal from the rest of its group. These three buffalo, however, have arranged themselves almost like a wall, making it difficult for the wolf to get to the buffalo calf.**

© Monty Sloan

P. Thompson

Gus Mills/Licaone Fund

▶ These wolves are all howling together. Howling is a way to get the group excited and ready to go to hunt.

© Monty Sloan

▼ Deer are often prey for wolves, but they can be difficult to catch.

What do wolves eat?

Although wolves can eat many different types of food, their main diet is large grass-eaters: moose, deer, elk, and caribou. Wolves will also eat garbage, dead animals, and small prey, like mice and rabbits.

Jane Packard

© Monty Sloan

◀ Where there is water there is food. These gray wolves may have come to the lake to look for a snack, such as this swan.

► Gray wolves can hunt small animals by pouncing on them. Wolves learn how to hunt like this when they are just pups.

◄ There are many times during hunting when no one ends up getting the food.

► As this mouse jumps out of the snow, the wolf pounces on it, playing with it, as a cat would. This wolf must not be hungry, since it hasn't eaten the mouse yet.

© Monty Sloan

33

What else do canids eat?

Some species, such as the red fox and coyote are often seen picking through garbage for meals. Depending on the species, wolf relatives eat insects, berries, meat, fish, mice, and just about anything they can find.

Suzanne Yin

◄ This coyote is drinking out of a milk carton it found on the side of the road. Scientists call coyotes "opportunists," since they take advantage of any opportunity to get a meal.

▼ The golden jackals in Turkey will often eat sea turtle eggs and the hatching turtles themselves.

◄ This red fox was photographed in Alaska and it was probably feeding on marine animals found in tidal pools.

Bernd Würsig

André Landry/Institute of Marine Life Sciences

What do kit foxes eat?

The kit fox is found in the deserts of California. Some of its prey are small snakes, lizards, birds, insects, and kangaroo rats.

▶ **The blunt-nosed leopard lizard is a prey of the kit fox in California. Both the kit fox and this lizard are endangered species.**

Rosalie Faubion/Bureau of Reclamation—California

Erik D. Stoops

▲ **A rattlesnake seems like an animal you'd want to stay away from, but coyotes—like many people—think rattlesnake makes a good meal.**

Do wolves ever hunt together with other types of animal?

One type of wild dog working with another type is probably not something that happens very often. Sometimes coyotes and badgers can be seen hunting side by side, but this is not "working together" as animals in a pack do.

Dick George/Phoenix Zoo

Pam Lennon/The Living Desert

▲ **A badger may attempt to dig out a meal while a coyote waits on the other side of the hole to catch any animal that tries to escape.**

35

Is a wolf a scavenger?

A scavenger cleans meat from bones of dead animals. You can think of scavengers as the cleanup crew after a big dinner, making sure no food is wasted. Jackals are often scavengers; wolves sometimes scavenge.

▶ **The black-backed jackal will sometimes follow lions, hoping to steal a meal.**

How much food can a wolf eat?

Wolves can eat up to 14–18 pounds (6–8 kg) of food at one time.

▶ **This wolf seems to be telling the other wolf to stay away until it has finished eating.**

Do wolves eat fruit?

Wolves and their relatives will eat fruit, with some eating it as a large part of their diet. Foxes eat fruit, such as berries, when meat is hard to find. The maned wolf has a diet that is almost exclusively fruit.

◀ **Most of the maned wolf's diet is a fruit found in Brazil that the locals call "wolf's fruit."**

Do wolves hide food?

Many wolf relatives, like jackals, foxes, and sometimes wolves themselves, bury food left over after a meal. This is called a **cache** (cash). A hole is dug by using both the paws and the muzzle. Foxes may wait a few weeks before returning to the spot to eat the stashed food.

How does a wolf pack choose its victim?

A wolf pack will test a herd of deer by chasing them. The weaker animals, which are either young, old, or sick, usually are not able to keep up with the other animals, and are noticed quickly by the wolves.

Do wolves get fat?

Wolves usually have to worry about not getting *enough* to eat. A wolf wouldn't have much of a chance to get fat, since it is constantly on the go, hunting food.

▲ Wolves do not mind being in water. In fact, wolves even follow escaping deer into the water to catch them.

▶ When it gets tough to find food and wolves are starving, the organization of the pack may start to break down and wolves within a pack may fight with each other.

◀ Snow conditions are an important factor during hunts. Success depends on how deep, soft, or compacted the snow is. The wolf moves around faster on hard, packed-together snow.

▲ Kills are often made by chasing an animal, such as this buffalo, and then jumping and biting it on the rump and sides. Sometimes the nose and shoulders are also the target.

WOLF REPRODUCTION

Being in a family is one of the most important parts of life to a wolf. By having a family and making sure the pups survive, every wild dog is able to make sure part of him/her lives to be part of future generations of wild dogs. Do wolves baby-sit? Why do puppies play? Do wolves make good parents? Discover what it's like to be a young pup growing up.

◄ Not all wolves in a pack will bear pups, but they work together to take care of the young.

Do wolves have mates for life?

Yes. A mated pair of wolves will try to stay together for life. When a mate dies, the single wolf will have to try to find another mate.

▼ Wild dogs, such as these Patagonian foxes, nuzzle one another as a sign of affection.

How do coyotes pick mates?

During certain times of the year, depending on the species, male coyotes show off and try to attract the females' attention. A female may have two or more males following her around at this time. After a few weeks many of the males lose interest, while one male may stick around. The female then mates with the male.

Bernd Würsig

How do wolves mate?

Once the female is willing to be mated with, the male climbs up on her back and inserts his reproductive organ into the female's. Wolves mate for about 20–30 minutes.

(Top right and bottom left) **These two wolves are mating.**

© Monty Sloan

How long is the female pregnant?

After mating, the female is pregnant for about nine weeks.

How old do wolves have to be to mate?

Wolves start mating when they are about four or five years old.

© Monty Sloan

What is a baby wolf called?

Wolf babies are usually called pups, or puppies. Baby foxes are called kits.

▶ These wolf puppies are about three weeks old. They have started to check out their surroundings. The smells and sounds are very interesting to them.

© Monty Sloan

How many pups does a mother wolf have?

Wolf mothers usually have four to six pups in a litter. Sometimes, as many as 10 pups are born at a time. Wolf pups weigh about a pound (0.5 kg), are about eight inches (20 cm) long, and are very dependent upon their mothers.

P.K. Anderson/American Society of Mammalogists

◀ Fox babies are called kits. These are kit fox youngsters.

41

Where are wolf puppies born?

Puppies are born in a den, which is often a small, dark place underground with a tunnel leading to it. Some dens are used year after year, but sometimes, a new den has to be dug by the mother. In other cases, a mother wolf will find some other animal's den, kick them out, and make it a little larger to suit herself.

© Wild Canid Survival and Research Center.

◄ **This Iranian gray wolf pup is poking his head out of his safe den.**

► **Wolf pups open their eyes when they are 11–15 days old. They don't open their eyes all of a sudden. What happens is that the closed eyes begin to see cracks of light, and every day the pups see more and more of their surroundings. Wolf pups are born in dens, which are very dark. When they are old enough, they begin to move around the den and to the outside world.**

Jane Packard

What do puppies eat?

When they are first born, pups only drink milk that they suck from their mother's nipples, like other mammals. Milk is not only a good source of vitamins and nutrients that are needed for the pups to grow up big and strong, but it also gives some protection to the puppies so they don't get sick as easily.

© Monty Sloan

A Murie/American Society of Mammalogists

▲ While the puppies are not able to move around well, the mother lies down so that they can reach her nipples.

◄ When the youngsters start getting bigger and are walking around, the mothers, like this red fox, stand up while their babies nurse.

43

What is weaning?

When pups are about three or four weeks old, they have their sharp baby teeth. These teeth can hurt the mother while the pups are nursing. At this time, while the pups are still nursing a little bit, the parents give them meat to chew and bones to gnaw. The time when pups are tasting meat, but still drinking their mother's milk, is called weaning.

How do wolves introduce meat to their pups?

Most wolves will swallow pieces of meat whole and then go back to their pups. The pups get very excited that they are going to get some food, so they begin to lick the mouth of the parent with the food. This helps make the parent regurgitate (cough up) the food, which the pups can then eat.

▲ **This little maned wolf pup will grow up to look just like its parents.**

◄ **This African wild dog pup is getting fed by the adult, who will cough up partially digested food from its stomach.**

▶ **These African wild dogs are getting ready to beg for some food. They beg by licking and biting the jaw of the adult.**

Do wolves make good parents?

Yes. Since the pups are born helpless, they really depend on their mothers to keep them warm, fed, clean, and safe. Father wolves are busy as well, bringing food for the mother while she is nursing the pups.

How do parents tell their pups apart?

They recognize individual pups by smell, voice, and personality. They also can tell pups apart by the markings on their fur.

Do wolves make good baby-sitters?

Yes. Adult and adolescent members of the pack often help take care of other pups by bringing them food, watching for danger, and playing with them. Some may teach the puppies how to catch their own food.

Jane Packard

► You can tell these pups apart by their spot patterns.

◄ Puppies can sometimes try an adult's patience.

A Maggi/Licaone Fund

J.G. Hall/American Society of Mammalogists

▲ Many mammal dads help very little, and sometimes not at all, in taking care of their babies. Jackal fathers will help the mothers to feed their offspring. Adolescent jackals often stay with their parents to help raise younger brothers and sisters.

How long do pups stay at the same den?

When the pups are about nine weeks old, they move to a new home. This place is like a den above the ground. It is a safe place for the pups to be left by themselves while the adults go hunting. The pups spend their time in the den playing with each other and resting.

Jane Packard

▲ This pup looks as if it's waiting for everyone to come home from hunting.

When do pups start hunting for their own food?

They will practice at first on things like grasshoppers, which they usually end up missing at first! But, practice makes perfect. The pups are usually about a year old before they get involved in the big hunts, and are actually good at them. When they are younger, the pups' bodies are not strong enough, and they do not have the right skills to be able to hunt fast and strong animals.

▶ This pup has many skills to learn before it's ready to become an adult.

Julian Center for Science and Education

Jane Packard

◀ When pups are young and need to be moved to a safer place, the mother or father will pick the pup up by the scruff of its neck (as a cat does with its kittens) and carry it there.

46

Jane Packard

Why do puppies play so much?

Puppies play for the same reason that we all do—it's fun! Rough and tumble also helps the puppies learn about their bodies (how far they can jump, etc.) as well as strengthening and coordinating their muscles for when they have to hunt and protect themselves against predators. Pups also practice hunting by pouncing on feathers and leaves that flutter down in the wild. During play the pups also learn about adult behavior.

▲ Wolf pups often play-fight. Play not only helps pups exercise and test their bodies, but it is also a good way for pups to bond with one another and establish dominance within the litter.

47

SELF-DEFENSE

Imagine that you are staring up at the face of an angry wolf with its large, sharp teeth and powerful paws and claws! This would scare just about any animal away. But the wolf is not always the toughest animal around. How do wolves protect themselves? Who are their enemies and why do they fight?

◄ A wolf living in a pack is safer than a single animal. Wolves can move fast and bite quickly to scare off enemies.

© Monty Sloan

◄ An angry wolf, threatening to attack, will pull its lips back, show its teeth, lay down its ears, and with its hair standing straight up, let out a deep growl.

How do wolves protect themselves?

According to scientists, wolves react differently depending on the situation. A wolf may choose to blend in with its surroundings in order to avoid a fight. It may also run away from a potential enemy. At other times, it will actively defend itself.

► Wolves work very hard to take care of their pups. Very protective, they will often growl and bark when the litter is in trouble. Another way is for the wolf to move away from where the puppies are and to attract attention to itself by barking.

© Monty Sloan

◄ These African wild dogs are harassing a pesky hyena to make him go away from their food, even though the hyena weighs about three times as much as the wild dog. A good bite on the bottom usually does the trick.

▼ Wolves and grizzly bears tend to avoid each other but will sometimes fight over a carcass.

Does a wolf have any enemies?

Yes, one of the biggest threats to a wolf is the human race. Wolves get their feet caught in traps, they are shot and poisoned, and for one reason only—fear. People tend to be afraid of wolves. Black, brown, and grizzly bears as well as mountain lions can also be a problem for adult wolves and their pups. Not only does a wolf have to be alert to animals on the ground, but from the air as well—birds of prey like eagles also watch for pups that wander away from the den.

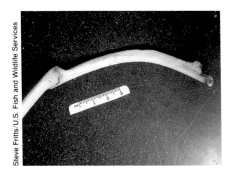

◄ This is the healed broken rib of a gray wolf. Wolves can easily get broken bones by a kick in the side or in the head by deer or moose hooves.

50

The deer is one of the wolf's favorite foods, but the deer's antlers can be a powerful and dangerous weapon.

▼ These African wild dogs may be looking out for lions or hyenas that could be near, threatening the group.

Dave Weller

Do wolves post lookouts?

Wolves and some of their relatives have members of their group or pack that act as lookouts. Some of these members take turns. When danger is near, the leader or the lookout will alert the others.

A. Maggi/Licaone Fund

Do wolf pups have any enemies?

Yes. Many animals have a taste for wolf pups. One of these is the hawk; another is the bobcat. A wolf pup can be an easy target.

© W.R. Elsberry

◀ With the ability to see for great distances, the red tail hawk can easily spot a wandering wolf pup and make a meal out of it.

Heather Bell

◀ Pups also have to watch out for big cats, like this bobcat.

Do wolves ever fight with one another?

Yes. If one wolf goes into another's territory, it will be attacked. What the wolves might do first is threaten each other. When they do this, their hair stands up and they bare their teeth. This takes less energy than fighting and is safer for any animal. If bluffing doesn't work, a real fight will result and can become violent. In many cases, one of the wolves is killed and even eaten.

Steve Fritts/U.S. Fish and Wildlife Service

▲ **This wolf was killed by other wolves, probably after coming into their territory.**

© Monty Sloan

◄ **These wolves are staring each other down trying to figure out whether there's going to be a fight. Sometimes just a look is enough to get the message to each other.**

WOLVES AND PEOPLE

Many people around the world fear wolves, and that's mostly because they don't understand them. But as a result of that fear, wolves are killed. How do scientists study wolves and their relatives? How are wolves important to nature? Read on and find some of the answers.

◀ **These Arctic foxes are scavenging through garbage.**

Are wolves important to nature?

Yes. Wolves help keep populations of grass-eaters, such as deer, healthy by weeding out the old, the weak, and the sick. This helps ensure that there will be enough food for the healthy, strong deer to eat.

▶ **In Isle Royale National Park on Lake Superior, biologists found that trees did not grow as much during some periods in the 1980s, when disease had reduced the number of wolves. Wolves keep populations of herbivores (like deer and moose) in check. When the wolf population was low, the herbivore population became large and the tree population suffered. You can see now that wolves play an important role in nature.**

Dick George/Phoenix Zoo

© Monty Sloan

▲ **Wolves play a very important role in nature by keeping a balance in the animal population.**

Elissif Andrews Brandon

Why are wolves hunted and killed?

Wolves and their relatives are killed by people for many different reasons. Hunters and poachers kill them for their fur because people pay large amounts of money for it. Some ranchers feel that the wolf is a pest because it feeds on their sheep and cattle. Another reason that wolves are killed is because people are afraid of them.

▼ **With more and more land being cleared away for farming and building, it gets harder for wolves to feed their families. These are the remains of a small calf that a pack of wolves ate.**

▼ **Out of 34 wild dog species, 21 are blamed for killing chickens, sheep, cattle, and goats. Wolves are also considered by some people to be competition for wild animals like deer. This gray wolf was shot illegally by a deer hunter.**

Steve Fritts/U.S. Fish and Wildlife Service

Steve Fritts/U.S. Fish and Wildlife Service

56

◄ The maned wolf is hunted for other reasons. One is because of superstition—its eyes, skin, and tail are said to have magic powers.

Wildlife World Zoo

► Many wolves are killed because people are afraid of what they don't understand. Through education and public awareness this might stop.

© Monty Sloan

What is a fur farm?

This is a place where animals, such as foxes, are raised for their fur. This means the fur did not come from an animal caught in a trap in the wild.

What is a pelt?

A pelt is the skin and fur of an animal, such as a wolf or fox. Pelts are used to make fur coats and other products that are sold to people who wear them as a fashion statement. Pelts are also used for hats, scarfs, mittens, and gloves.

Carter Neimaier/ U.S. Department of Agriculture

▲ Canid fur is used to make fur coats, trim parkas, and sometimes to make blankets. Pictured from left to right are pelts from a gray wolf, a coyote, and a red fox.

Bernd Würsig

◄ Around 20 species of wolves and their relatives are hunted or raised for their fur. The gray zorro, also known as the Patagonian gray fox, is one of those species.

Do wolves kill sheep and cattle?

Many ranchers blame wolves for dead chickens, sheep, goats, and cattle. Sometimes wolves are the culprit. Many times, however, it is **feral** (fair-uhl) dogs that kill domestic animals as well as wildlife. Feral dogs are homeless pets that turn wild.

© The Living Desert

◄ **Many people blame coyotes for dead sheep. However, often the sheep die for other reasons, and the coyotes find the dead bodies and eat them. This makes it look as if the coyote did the killing.**

© Monty Sloan

▲ **Domestic dogs, like this Great Pyrenees, are used to guard sheep against attack.**

Heather Bell

▲ **The kit fox is making a comeback. One of the reasons that there are so few kit foxes is that they accidentally get caught in traps or eat poisoned bait which is meant for coyotes and wolves.**

Heather Bell

▲ **The ground squirrel is a favorite food of kit foxes. Unfortunately, people poison the squirrels, since they feel that they are pests. Kit foxes eat these poisoned squirrels and die.**

Are wolves and their relatives killed in other ways?

Yes. Many species of wolves and their relatives get hit by cars on highways near where they live. The wolf doesn't see oncoming vehicles until it is too late. Wolves also die of natural causes, such as disease, weather, and injuries they get while hunting or fishing.

If I wanted to study wolves, what would I be?

People who study wolves and their relatives are called mammalogists. A mammalogist is a scientist who studies different species of mammals. Biologists and zoologists also study different species of wolves. Scientists with different specialties often work as a team to learn about wolves and how to save them.

P. Myers/American Society of Mammalogists

▲ This crab-eating fox was hit by a car. The biggest problem is that wild dogs probably don't see oncoming cars until too late.

◄ These scientists are called paleontologists. They are digging up fossil canid bones.

Helen and Dave Whistler

What is a radio collar?

A radio collar is a small radio tracking device that is on a collar and fits around the wolf's neck. This can provide information about where the wolf goes. Scientists can follow a radio-tracked wolf by airplane or by foot.

How do they put the radio collar on the wolf?

After the wolf is caught and given a tranquilizer to put it to sleep, it is fitted with the radio collar, which it wears during the study. This does not hurt the wolf.

▶ Researchers will be in constant contact with the Patagonian gray fox, but the fox won't be aware of it.

Steve Fritts/U.S. Fish and Wildlife Service

▲ These mammalogists are putting a radio collar on this sleeping wolf to help them learn more about wolves.

J.M. Chupasko

▲ This wolf pup, waking up from the anesthesia, has a new radio collar.

Warren E. Johnson

Steve Fritts/U.S. Fish and Wildlife Service

Steve Fritts/U.S. Fish and Wildlife Service

(left and above) **A researcher picks up radio signals from the wolf's collar using a hand-held or plane-carried antenna and receiver, the other part of the radio-tracking device.**

Steve Fritts/U.S. Fish and Wildlife Service

How else do scientists find wolves?

Scientists can follow wolf prints in the snow or mud. The fresher the print, the closer the wolf.

▶ Another way is for the scientist to howl out to the wolves in the area.

Steve Fritts/U.S. Fish and Wildlife Service

▲ **One way to track wolves is to follow their prints.**

How do scientists catch wolves?

Scientists use traps called leg-hold traps, which are buried in the ground and are baited with meat. The wolf steps right into this special trap and doesn't get hurt.

J.M. Chupasko

J.M. Chupasko

▲ This is a leg-hold trap that helps scientists catch wolves. This is the safest and best way to catch an adult wolf.

▲ The trap is already buried. Meat put nearby gets the wolf to step right into the trap.

▼ The trap is set, buried, and baited. Look closely. The trap is located in the small wood pieces.

J.M. Chupasko

What do scientists do with wolves they capture?

A captured wolf is put down with a tranquilizer dart. The wolf is weighed. Next, blood is drawn and put into test tubes.

The scientists clip on ear tags and might also measure the wolf's teeth. The wolf usually wakes up in about 30 minutes.

Steve Fritts/U.S. Fish and Wildlife Service

P. Rizzato/Licaone Fund

◄ This scientist is taking blood from an African wild dog. By testing the blood the scientist can figure out the type of disease the wild dog has and can discover its genetic makeup.

▲ It would be hard to weigh a wolf that was awake. So researchers dart the animal with a drug that makes it sleepy and not able to move around.

Steve Fritts/U.S. Fish and Wildlife Service

▲ This scientist measures this wolf's canine teeth. Some scientists are interested in finding out how big the teeth are at different stages of the wolf's development.

J.M. Chupasko

◄ Blood can be taken from an artery located in the neck or in the leg.

64

What are ear tags?

Scientists put ear tags on wolves so they can identify different individuals they study.

▶ **This wolf is now wearing ear tags that help the scientists identify it later on.**

Steve Fritts/U.S. Fish and Wildlife Service

What is a muzzle?

A muzzle is a device that is put over a wolf's mouth to protect the scientist from being bitten.

▶ **This dingo pup has a muzzle on, so it can't bite anyone. Its feet have been bound, so it can't claw, or run away. Notice the metal tag in its right ear.**

P. Thomson

Have wolves ever attacked people?

Wolves tend to be shy and usually try to avoid people. Very few people have ever been attacked by a wolf without a good reason.

How can I help wolves?

Many people donate time or money to organizations that protect animals all over the world. You can also help by telling your friends to learn more about wolves and not to fear them.

Licaone Fund

▲ These are the people who started the Licaone Fund, an organization dedicated to saving the African wild dog. Researchers and non-scientists help educate the public about these wolves and their relatives, trying to reduce the threats these animals face.

Are there any endangered wolves?

Gray wolves, along with a number of other canids, are having trouble surviving. The most endangered dog species are the African wild dog, the red wolf, and the Ethiopian wolf, which are facing extinction.

© Wild Canid Survival and Research Center

◄ The Mexican wolf, a type of gray wolf, is endangered. It became endangered because of habitat destruction and illegal hunting.

▶ There are few red wolves in the wild. The best place to see one is at a conservation center.

Patrick Kelly

◀ Maybe someday, you'll be lucky enough to see African wild dogs in the wild, roaming free and safe.

G. Mills/Licaone Fund

What is being done to help wolves and their relatives survive?

Zoos and other organizations are breeding endangered wolves so they may be returned to the wild. Laws such as CITES and the Endangered Species Act make it illegal to harm, capture, or kill wolves without permission. CITES, which stands for Convention on International Trade in Endangered Species, puts limits on international trade that threatens the survival of a canid species or population. More than 80 nations observe this law.

▼ Red wolves are bred in conservation centers to be reintroduced into the wild. The red wolf was once extinct in the wild but it is starting to make a comeback very slowly. The first red wolf was reintroduced in 1987 in northeastern North Carolina.

© Wild Canid Survival and Research Center

How were wild dogs important in culture?

Many fairy tales and children's stories present the wolf as an evil animal. However, some ancient cultures believed that wolves and their relatives were quite powerful. The ancient Egyptians worshiped the jackal-headed god Anubis. Native Americans revere wolves and their relatives as being mystical and having great powers. Symbols of these wolves can be seen on walls and figure prominently in Native American artwork.

Claudio Sillero-Zubiri

▲ **The biggest threat to the Ethiopian wolf is the domestic dog. Dogs are** used to guard cattle and sheep. Dogs compete with wolves for food, transmit disease (such as rabies), and crossbreed with wolves. Crossbreeding threatens to make the Ethiopian wolf extinct genetically.

Karen Sausman / © The Living Desert

◄ **Fennec foxes are often caught by Bedouins (nomadic Arab tribes in the Arabian, Syrian, and North African deserts) to be sold as pets.**

GREAT WOLVES & THEIR RELATIVES

Did you know that there are 34 different types of wild dog? They are all of different shapes and sizes, and some are very strange-looking. Which is the largest? Which is the smallest? How are they named? Read on and find these and other answers.

▶ **The gray wolf is a popular and often-studied wolf species.**

Dick George/Phoenix Zoo

When were the first wolves domesticated?

The wolf was one of the first animals domesticated. Many scientists believe that wolves were domesticated some 20,000 years ago to help people find and catch food, as well as warn of danger. Hence the saying, "The dog is man's best friend."

▲ **All pet dogs are descendants of the wolf.**

Do wolves make good pets?

No. Most people do not know how to take good care of them. It is also important to remember that wild animals can carry diseases that are dangerous to people. Many laws prohibit people from keeping wolves as pets.

How are wolves named?

Scientists called taxonomists help identify animals and name them. Each species has two parts in its name. The first word is called the genus and second is the species. These names are used by all scientists the world over. An example is *Canis lupus*, the gray wolf's scientific name.

What is a family, a genus, and a species of wild dog?

A *family* is a group of wild dogs and their relatives that share similar features. A *genus* is a smaller, more closely related group in the same family. A *species* is a specific kind of wild dog. There may be many *genera* (more than one genus) in a family and also many different species in a genus. The scientific name for the gray wolf is *Canis lupus*. For example:

The **family** of wild dogs is Canidae.

A **genus** of Canidae is *Canis*.

A **species** of *Canis* is *lupus*.

How do scientists classify wolves and their relatives?

The easiest way to explain this is to show how to classify a wild dog. Let's try to classify a gray wolf.

Kingdom—Animalia (animals)

Phylum—Chordata (vertebrates are animals with backbones)

Class—Mammalia (mammals)

Order—Carnivora (carnivores)

Family—Canidae (wild dogs)

Genus—Canis (coyote, jackal, wolf, dingo, and domestic dog)

Species—lupus (the gray wolf)

▲ **The red wolf is named for its fur color.**

What is a coyote?

Coyotes are found in North America and Central America. They are smaller than wolves. A coyote has a more pointed muzzle than a wolf and large ears that point outwards.

▶ **The coyote's nickname is the "brush wolf" in part because it looks like a small wolf.**

72

What is a hyena?

Hyenas may look like wolves, but they are not relatives. A hyena has a thick muzzle with powerful jaws, and large ears and eyes. The reason African wild dogs and hyenas look familiar is because they both live in open areas.

▶ These spotted hyenas may look like dogs, but they are actually more closely related to cats.

Hans Kruuk

What is a jackal?

Jackals are small (weighing an average 24 lbs, or 11 kg) slender wolf relatives that have large, standing ears. There are four species of jackal found in Africa, southeastern Europe, and South Asia. The word "jackal" means sneaky and cowardly. Jackals hunt for most of their food, but will also steal food from other predators.

▶ The San Joaquin kit fox is found in the California desert. It lives in places where people drill for oil. This not only exposes it to possible oil spills, but to loud noise as well.

What is a fox?

Foxes are small wild dogs with pointed muzzles, large ears, and long bushy tails. There are 21 species of fox. Unlike wolves, foxes are not very social animals; they hunt and travel by themselves.

Heather Bell

What about zorro?

The word "zorro" means fox in Spanish. Foxes that live in South America are called zorros by the local people.

M.A. Rosenthal/American Society of Mammalogists

▲ The small-eared dog makes its home in the rain forests of the Amazon.

73

What is an African wild dog?

This species, also known as the painted wolf or the Cape hunting dog, has a coat that looks like a bright patchwork of yellow, black, white, and gray blotches. They are a distinctive species with large, rounded ears, long legs, and a bushy tail. African wild dogs live in packs, and are one of the world's most successful predators. They are one of the most endangered of the canids.

What is a dhole?

Dholes are found throughout eastern and central Asia. They have rounded ears and long, bushy tails. They live in packs and hunt during the cool parts of the day. Dholes bite their prey (buffalo and deer) as they chase them.

G. Mills/Licaone Fund

▲ **African wild dogs are the most colorful of all wolves and their relatives. Each has a different pattern of colored spots.**

Roland Wirth, courtesy of Colin Groves

◄ **There are two types of dhole; one lives in India and one in China. This is a Chinese dhole. It has thicker, redder fur than its cousin in India.**

74

What is a dingo?

A long time ago, the dingo was tamed by the native people of Australia, the Aborigines. After some time, the dingo went back to living in the wild.

▶ **Some scientists do not consider the dingo to be a "wild" wolf relative, because it was tamed by people long ago.**

K. Kutunidisz/American Society of Mammalogists

Colin Graves

◀ **The dingo is the only wild dog family member that lives in Australia.**

What is the largest canid?

The gray wolf is the biggest of all the dog family, weighing from 35 lbs (16 kg) to a hefty 132 pounds (80 kg) and measuring up to 32 inches (81 cm) at the shoulder. Females are usually smaller than the males. To get an idea of how big a wolf is, compare it to a good-sized German Shepherd dog, which stands about 28 inches (72 cm) at the shoulder and weighs a little over 100 pounds (45.5 kg).

▲ The large size of the gray wolf helps it when it hunts large animals like deer and bison. Its size may also help scare off potential enemies.

Which is the smallest wolf relative?

The Fennec fox is the smallest, weighing in at less than 3 pounds (1.5 kg). It would take almost 60 Fennec foxes to equal the weight of a gray wolf.

◄ The Fennec fox is the smallest member of the dog family.

What is the strangest-looking wolf relative?

There are a few very unusual-looking species. The maned wolf has really long legs that make it look as if it's walking on stilts. The bat-eared fox has very large ears that look too big for its head.

▶ **The bat-eared fox has some of the largest ears of any wolf relative. The bat-eared fox uses its big ears to find its prey—insects.**

J. Anderson/American Society of Mammalogists

Wildlife World Zoo

◀ **The maned wolf has a red coat and very long legs. Did you know that its back legs are longer than its front legs? Long legs make it easier for the maned wolf o see over tall grasses.**

Can any wolves or their relatives climb trees?

Most can't climb, and those that try don't usually do a very good job of it. Gray foxes are the champion climbers. They are so good at climbing trees, they often use trees as temporary hideouts. They can do this because they have long, sharp claws that are curved like those of cats.

◄ Gray foxes can hide out in trees, looking for food or for animals that may want to eat them.

▶ Most wild dogs are not good climbers. The gray wolf is not a good climber.

What are the rarest canids?

The red wolf is one of the rarest wolves in the world, with fewer than 100 in the wild. The Ethiopian wolf is very rare because of human pressures. One of the biggest is habitat destruction.

▶ **The Ethiopian wolf lives high in the mountains of Ethiopia. Little is known about this species.**

Claudio Sillero-Zubiri

© Wild Canid Research and Survival Center

◀ **The rarest wolf is the red wolf. Red wolves at one time were found throughout the wetlands of the southeastern United States.**

Acknowledgments

This book would not have been possible without the help of the following fine researchers, organizations, and photographers: American Society of Mammalogists (and associated photographers); Heather Bell & Patrick Kelly, San Joaquin Valley Endangered Species Recovery Planning Program; Lawrence G. Barnes, Natural History Museum of Los Angeles County; Marc Bekoff, University of Colorado; Elisif Andrews Brandon; J.M. Chupasko; W.R. Elsberry; Rosalie Faubion, Bureau of Reclamation in California; Steve Fritts, U.S. Fish and Wildlife Service; Todd Fuller; Dick George, Phoenix Zoo; Colin Groves; Laura Handoca, IUCN Canid Specialist Group; Deborah A. Jefferson; Thomas A. Jefferson; Warren E. Johnson; Julian Center for Science and Education; Hans Kruuk; André Landry, Institute of Marine Life Sciences; Licaone Fund; The Living Desert; Keith Mullin; Carter Niemaier, U.S. Dept. of Agriculture; Jane Packard, Texas A&M University; George Schaller; Claudio Sillero Zubiri, IUCN Canid Specialist Group; Monty Sloan, Wolf Park; Fiona Sunquist; Peter Thomson; David Weller; Helen and David P. Whistler, Natural History Museum of Los Angeles County; Wild Canid Survival and Research Center; Wildlife World Zoo; Bernd Würsig; Suzanne Yin. Illustrations were provided by Frank Barath.

We would also like to thank the many people who helped put us in contact with sources of information and photographs; without them this book would not be complete. We are grateful to Claudio Sillero-Zubiri, IUCN Canid Specialist Group; Theresa Stefancik, Licaone Fund; Tom Tomasi, children's science book reviewer; and Sheila Barry and Hannah Steinmetz, Sterling Publishing Co., for their thoughtful reviews that improved this book. Last, but certainly not least, we thank our families and friends, who put up with us during the craziness of completing this book.

Index